BECOMING A PRO
BASKETBALL
PLAYER

BY THERESE SHEA

Gareth Stevens
PUBLISHING

Please visit our website, www.garethstevens.com. For a free color catalog of all our high-quality books, call toll free 1-800-542-2595 or fax 1-877-542-2596.

Library of Congress Cataloging-in-Publication Data

Shea, Therese.
Becoming a pro basketball player / by Therese Shea.
p. cm. — (Going pro)
Includes index.
ISBN 978-1-4824-2058-6 (pbk.)
ISBN 978-1-4824-2057-9 (6-pack)
ISBN 978-1-4824-2059-3 (library binding)
1. Basketball — Juvenile literature. I. Shea, Therese. II. Title.
GV885.1 S54 2015
796.32—d23

First Edition

Published in 2015 by
Gareth Stevens Publishing
111 East 14th Street, Suite 349
New York, NY 10003

Copyright © 2015 Gareth Stevens Publishing

Designer: Nicholas Domiano
Editor: Therese Shea

Photo credits: Cover, p. 1 Erik Isakson/Blend Images/Getty Images; p. 5 Ronald Martinez/Getty Images Sport/Getty Images; p. 6 (inset) Doug Pensinger/Getty Images Sport/Getty Images; p. 7 Daniel H. Bailey/ Photolibrary/Getty Images; p. 9 (red flag) Alhovik/Shutterstock.com; p. 9 (boy) Alexander Raths/ Shutterstock.com; p. 9 (basketball court) spirit of america/Shutterstock.com; p. 11 Jamie Roach/ Shutterstock.com; p. 13 Lexington Herald-Leader/McClatchy Tribune/Getty Images; p. 15 Mike Fuentes/AP Photos; p. 17 Jim McLsaac/Getty Images Sport/Getty Images; p. 19 Orlando Sentinel/McClatchy-Tribune/ Getty Images; p. 21 Aris Messinis/AFP/Getty Images; p. 23 (main) Bob Levey/Getty Images Sport/Getty Images; p. 23 (inset) Thearon W. Henderson/Getty Images Sport/Getty Images; p. 25 Darin Oswald/AP Photos; p. 26 (inset) Robert Sullivan/AFP/Getty Images; p. 27 Stephen Dunn/Getty Images Sport/Getty Images; p. 29 MCT/McClatchy-Tribune/Getty Images.

Printed in the United States of America

CPSIA compliance information: Batch #CW15GS: For further information contact Gareth Stevens, New York, New York at 1-800-542-2595.

CONTENTS

Words in the glossary appear in **bold** type the first time they are used in the text.

UNDER PRESSURE

It's the basketball finals. Your team is down by a point with 1 second to go. You're standing at the foul line. If you make both shots, your team can win. The **referee** hands you the basketball. You take a breath, aim, and **release** the ball. SWISH! The crowd is on their feet now. Just one more shot. You take another breath, aim, and release . . .

Do you have the ability to perform in high-pressure situations like this? Do you think you have the skills to become a **professional** basketball player? It's not an easy road, but there are things young athletes can do now to give themselves a chance to make it big.

ACCESSIBLE SPORT

Anyone with a basketball can play basketball. People can learn and practice how to dribble and run with the ball by themselves. Schools and neighborhoods have basketball courts so beginners can get skilled at shooting from different places on the court. Many schools and neighborhoods also have leagues for people of all ages and skill levels.

Some basketball games are decided by a single point. Making foul shots and keeping cool in high-pressure situations are key parts of the sport.

THE FUNDAMENTALS

Most professional basketball players spent time on the court when they were young. They learned the fundamentals of the game in a community league or on an elementary school team. Every basketball player, no matter their position, needs to know how to play offense and defense. They need to rebound, dribble, shoot, and pass well, too. They must have both endurance and **agility**. Basketball players also work on footwork to trick opponents and beat them down the court.

A player needs to be very good at all these things, but must excel in at least one to stand out among all the other skilled basketball players.

TIM DUNCAN

LATE BLOOMERS

Not all pro basketball players are on the court at a young age. For example, **power forward** superstar Tim Duncan didn't begin to play until his freshman year of high school. Before that, though, Duncan was an excellent athlete in a different sport—swimming. However, most people need years of practice to shine in this sport.

Many pros suggest playing against people who are better than you are. That way, you'll know your weaknesses and learn what skills to focus on.

HIGH SCHOOL

In high school, basketball players sharpen their skills against other players on competing high school teams or in other **amateur** basketball associations such as the AAU (Amateur Athletic Union). Many players are first noticed at high school or amateur team tournaments by college coaches and **recruiters** who are looking for up-and-coming players for their squads.

It's not only important to be great on the court, though. It's also necessary to follow the rules of conduct on and off the court and perform well in school. Many high school athletes compete for college athletic **scholarships**, and these opportunities require a minimum grade point average as well as certain coursework.

WALK-ONS

College can't offer enough scholarships to recruit a full basketball team. "Walk-ons" are players who didn't receive scholarships or get recruited to a college. They first "walk on" the court at tryouts. There have been players who were walk-ons who ended up in the pros, such as Scottie Pippen.

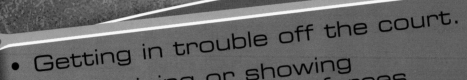

AVOID RED FLAGS

- Getting in trouble off the court.
- Complaining or showing disrespect toward referees or coaches.
- Low GPA.
- Bad language, poor attitude, or posting inappropriate materials online.
- Showing up late.
- Showing off or bragging.

Getting cut from the high school team doesn't have to be the end of the road for an athlete. Michael Jordan didn't make his varsity team in his sophomore year. That made him try harder to succeed the next year.

A high school basketball coach is probably the best resource to launch a college career. High school coaches often have connections to college coaches. They can contact schools for their players, helping them get noticed or even recruited for a team.

Some professionals suggest that players create a basketball **résumé** in high school. On it, they should list contact information, game **statistics**, and academic record, such as grade point average and national test scores. They should also prepare a video of game highlights showing themselves as "difference makers." Players can send these to a basketball program themselves, but it may get more attention coming from a coach.

COLLEGE CAMPS

Colleges may put on camps for players of all ages to improve their skills. These camps usually cost money to attend, so players should make sure they compare what camps are promising as well as whether they will help in the recruitment process. Some camps are by invitation only, such as the NBPA (National Basketball Players Association) Top 100 Camp; coaches must recommend players.

If you're ready to commit to a school that's recruiting you, you'll sign a national letter of intent, which means you're intending on going to that school. Other colleges aren't allowed to contact you after that.

THE NCAA

The NCAA (National Collegiate Athletic Association) is the most well-known organization that oversees college athletics in the United States and Canada. It enforces rules so that players can succeed as students as well as athletes. The NCAA governs athletics in over 1,200 colleges and universities, which are divided into three divisions.

However, many great professional players attend non-NCAA colleges. These schools allow overlooked and developing players a chance to grow and shine. For example, NAIA (National Association of Intercollegiate Athletics) school Southeastern Oklahoma State University produced all-star Dennis Rodman. It was there that NBA (National Basketball Association) scouts noticed his collegiate career.

THE WNBA

Most WNBA (Women's National Basketball Association) players come from NCAA schools. There are particularly strong women's basketball programs at the University of Connecticut and the University of Tennessee. Other notable schools include the University of Notre Dame, Duke University, Stanford University, Baylor University, and the University of South Carolina. The WNBA also recruits from other countries, such as Australia, Sweden, and Brazil.

In 2014, the University of Connecticut Huskies won both the men's and women's NCAA national championships.

THE AAU

The Amateur Athletic Union (AAU) is another way for amateur athletes to gain experience in their sports. AAU basketball tournaments are especially of interest to college coaches. Championship teams often have many players who end up in competitive NCAA Division I schools. The AAU gives players exposure to a national spotlight that they might not get on their high school team.

Chris Paul, Carmelo Anthony, Lamar Odom, and Anthony Davis are current NBA stars who got noticed in the AAU. Brittney Griner and Maya Moore, two number-one picks in the WNBA draft, were also AAU stars. The AAU is sometimes called "pro prep."

SCOUTS

Scouts are people trained to spot talent in athletes. Scouts travel all over the world and watch many games to discover the best athletes. They look for skill level as well as speed and strength. One NBA scout said he looked for "basketball IQ," which means an ability to make the right play at the right time.

The AAU is divided into age-appropriate teams. College basketball programs use AAU tournaments to scout players in a central location.

SKIP COLLEGE?

You're probably familiar with some remarkable players who skipped college and were recruited directly to the NBA, such as LeBron James, Kobe Bryant, and Kevin Garnett. Most players can't make the jump to pro basketball that easily, though. And NCAA rules now state that players must be at least 19 years old and a year past their high school graduating class before turning pro.

Some players are choosing to go to Europe to play in professional basketball leagues until they're **eligible** for the NBA. There, they can get contracts to play for several years as well as money from **endorsements**.

CAREER-ENDING INJURIES

A basketball player's worst fear is getting an injury so severe they can no longer play. It's a good idea to have an alternate plan in case of a career-ending injury. Earning a college degree while playing basketball is a good way to prepare for the future. Some players hold degrees in sports management and other related fields.

LeBron James (left) and Kevin Garnett (right) made the transition to the NBA easily. However, that's not the norm for most young players coming into the league.

THE DRAFT

The NBA Draft is the event in which NBA teams pick the best available players who are eligible to go pro. There are two rounds in which each team gets one pick.

Before the draft, players are invited to a camp to run drills and play games to show off their skills to NBA team managers, coaches, and scouts. Teams may invite players to work out with them as well. The players may even be asked to take tests so teams can get a sense of their personality and character. Teams don't want to waste their draft pick on a player who isn't going to improve their team.

WHOM TO CHOOSE?

At the draft, teams may choose a player to fill an open or weak position on their team. They may select someone because he or she is the best all-around player available even if they have a good player who plays that position. They may even choose someone so they can trade for another player.

Before the draft, players are ranked in order of ability.

THE EUROPEAN CONNECTION

Sometimes, players are drafted into the NBA and WNBA, but still don't make the team. That happened to Darryl Middleton, a power forward at Baylor University. After he was cut by the Atlanta Hawks, Middleton decided to play in Europe. He began his career in Turkey, but returned to the United States to play in the NBA summer league. However, he then went back to Europe and became one of the most respected American players in the European leagues.

Some famous European players have been drafted into the NBA and WNBA, too. These include Tony Parker (France), Pau Gasol (Spain), Dirk Nowitzki (Germany), Lauren Jackson (Australia), Penny Taylor (Australia), and Erika de Souza (Brazil).

OTHER LEAGUES

The Euroleague is a professional basketball league across Europe. Other leagues play within a country, such as Ireland's Superleague. Asia, Africa, and Australia also support at least one basketball league. In the United States and Canada, there are organizations besides the NBA and the WNBA, such as the American Basketball Association, the National Basketball Association of Canada, and the Women's Blue Chip Basketball League.

Some basketball players like playing in Europe so much they decide to stay. That's why Darryl Middleton still lives there.

ALWAYS DEVELOPING

Playing with and against the best players in the world, players must "up" their game to win and keep their position on the court. They work with athletic trainers, strength and conditioning coaches, and dieticians to help them perfect their bodies and their skills.

Trainers can help even great players improve. For example, Chris Paul is a point guard about 5 feet 11 inches (180 cm) tall. That's not tall for a basketball player. However, once he turned pro, Paul focused on strengthening his legs to increase his vertical jump so he could shoot over taller players. He now jumps an amazing 38 inches (96.5 cm)!

EAT LIKE A LAKER

Doctor and dietician Cate Shanahan changed the Lakers' eating habits forever. Shanahan saw Dwight Howard performing poorly and linked it to his diet. She worked to improve the team's food choices, which meant avoiding sugar, processed foods, and unhealthy oils. Howard's energy levels soared as well as his endurance. Guard Steve Nash even credited the new diet for helping heal a broken leg.

CHRIS PAUL

Though nicknamed "Superman," Dwight Howard has had to work hard to maintain his high level of play.

THE D-LEAGUE

If players aren't ready for NBA action, they may have a chance of staying pro before getting cut. The NBA minor league is called the NBA Development League, or D-League. The D-League allows NBA teams to give their less experienced players increased playing time. Even superstars may play a few games in the league as they recover from injuries. The D-League also holds open tryouts, unlike the NBA, so anyone can have a shot at making the team.

More than 140 players in the NBA today have played in the development league at some point. That's over 30 percent of team rosters!

OPEN TRYOUTS

Unlike the NBA, some WNBA teams have open tryouts. However, women must have graduated from college or be 4 years past their high school graduation. They also must have had 2 years of professional experience playing basketball in another league. The goal of participants is to get an invitation to a team's training camp.

The D-League currently consists of
17 teams that play 50 games a season.

TRUE STORIES OF GOING PRO

Jeremy Lin played very well in high school and college but didn't have the flashiness of many other basketball recruits. NBA scouts didn't notice Lin, and he went undrafted in 2010. However, after playing on the Dallas Mavericks summer league team, Lin got an offer from the Golden State Warriors. He still seemed unremarkable and was passed to the Mavericks and then to the Knicks in 2011.

In New York, Lin didn't play much at first and knew he was about to be cut. However, he finally got a chance with the failing team. The Knicks went 7-0 once Lin earned his place on the court. He played so well he sparked "Linsanity" among fans.

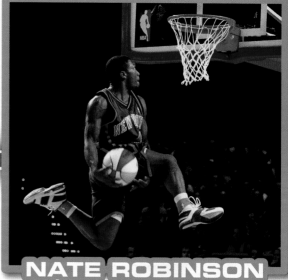

NATE ROBINSON

HOW TALL?

The average height in the NBA is 6 feet 7 inches (201 cm). However, shorter players have excelled. At 5 feet 3 inches (160 cm), longtime guard for the Charlotte Hornets Tyrone "Muggsy" Bogues was the shortest player ever. Point guard Nate Robinson is 5 feet 9 inches (175 cm) and has won three slam-dunk competitions.

At Harvard University, Lin became the first player in Ivy League history to record 1,450 points, 450 rebounds, 400 assists, and 200 steals. Before he got his break with the Knicks, he had started thinking about playing in Europe or even ending his career.

After an amazing high school career in Delaware, Elena Delle Donne accepted a scholarship to play for the top-ranked University of Connecticut. However, Donne quickly realized she wanted to be home, helping care for her disabled sister Lizzie. She took a huge risk and took the year off from basketball.

When Donne began playing again, this time at the nearby University of Delaware, she returned to her outstanding level of play. After entering the WNBA as the second pick in the draft, Donne was the 2013 Rookie of the Year.

Both Jeremy Lin and Elena Delle Donne are reminders that there's more than one path to a pro career. Besides skill, pros need great strength of character to survive on the court.

TOUGH ODDS

Even if you're a great player, the odds of making it to the pros are discouraging. One source says that 0.03 percent of high school players enter the NBA. That means 3 out of every 10,000 players. However, odds can be beaten. The best players keep trying to improve and up their game.

Donne (left) won her first AAU championship at age 12. Her 2,818 career points set a record for Delaware high school basketball history. Her 3,039 college career points are fifth in women's NCAA history.

GLOSSARY

agility: being able to move quickly and easily

amateur: someone who does something without pay

eligible: able to be chosen for something

endorsement: the act of supporting a product, especially for money

power forward: in basketball, a forward whose size and strength are used mainly to control play near the basket

professional: earning money from an activity that many people do for fun

recruiter: one whose job is to form a team by getting people to join

referee: a person who makes sure that players act according to the rules of a sport

release: to let go

résumé: a short paper describing a list of achievements

scholarship: money awarded to a student to pay for their education

statistics: information that can be related in numbers

FOR MORE INFORMATION

Books

Doeden, Matt. *The Best of Pro Basketball.* Mankato, MN: Capstone Press, 2010.

Latimer, Clay. *VIP Pass to a Pro Basketball Game Day: From the Locker Room to the Press Box (and Everything in Between).* Mankato, MN: Capstone Press, 2011.

Simmons, Bill. *The Book of Basketball: The NBA According to the Sports Guy.* New York, NY: Ballantine/ESPN Books, 2009.

Websites

SLAM 500 Greatest NBA Players of All Time
www.basketball-reference.com/awards/
slam_500_greatest.html
Check out the stats of the best NBA players ever.

WNBA.com
www.wnba.com
Find the biographies of your favorite WNBA players.

INDEX